Civil Twilight

Poems by
Anique Sara Taylor

BLUE LIGHT PRESS ◆ 1ST WORLD PUBLISHING

SAN FRANCISCO ◆ FAIRFIELD ◆ DELHI

Winner, 2022 Blue Light Poetry Prize
Civil Twilight
Copyright ©2023, Anique Sara Taylor

All rights reserved. Printed in the United States of America. No part of this book may be used or reproduced in any manner whatsoever without written permission except in the case of brief quotations embodied in critical articles and reviews. For information contact:

BLUE LIGHT PRESS
www.bluelightpress.com
bluelightpress@aol.com

1ST WORLD PUBLISHING
PO Box 2211
Fairfield, IA 52556
www.1stworldpublishing.com

BOOK & COVER DESIGN
Melanie Gendron
melaniegendron999@gmail.com

COVER ART
Anique Sara Taylor

AUTHOR PHOTO
Charlene McLaughlin-Eisenkraft

FIRST EDITION

Library of Congress Cataloging-in-Publication Data

ISBN: 978-1-4218-3539-6

Civil Twilight

Civil Twilight
When Earth's Surface Is Neither Completely Light Nor Dark
Sun's Geometric Center Is 6° Below Earth's Horizon
And Only the Brightest Stars Can Be Seen

for
My Father

Contents

Incandescent Constellations 1
Birthstone Harvest 2
Dangerous Chambers 3
Luminous Anarchy 4
Transient Promise 5
Mosaic Observations 6
Perpetual Suburbia 7
Invisible Cobwebs 8
Thursday's Child 9
Quicksilver Lilies 10
Sassafras Meadows 11
Speculation Pavilion 12
Asperity Dispensary 13
Harlequin Taproot 14
Revelation Commission 15
Necessary Calendula 16
Honeysuckle Jasmine 17
Innumerable Halos 18
Captive Harvest 19
Bittersweet Discernment 20
Shimmering Crossbow 21
Latticed Partitions 22
Between Stepping Stones 23
Ethereal Refractions 24
A Contagion of Miracles 25
Divisions of Solitude 26
Fireworks of the Field 27
Seagrass Airship 28
Space Capsule Chronicles 29
Civil Twilight 30

Continuing Thanks Always To: 33
About the Author 35

Incandescent Constellations

The moon's upper limb rises
as the sun's hesitant center sinks six
degrees below the horizon. Swim
back from the sunset. Now only
the brightest stars will ever be enough.

Birthstone Harvest

Toppling through air east of hope,
continuous filaments crust my eyes
and mouth. Even lying featherless
in dusk, I carve each day with care.
Nowhere is the tempo this reckless.

Dangerous Chambers

Showers, soon thunderstorms threaten.
A hollow in high weeds tunnels
into rubble & dust. If I could burrow
inside as white-tailed rabbits do.
Vanish. As loved ones do. Like you.

Luminous Anarchy

Driving too fast, slipping uneasy into
darkness, I foolishly hunt for shelter
to hide from flying debris. Shivering
before sunrise, shy mouth nailed shut,
does anybody know how to grieve?

Transient Promise

My clouded fingers shadow your
face. A deserted passageway between
buildings, I collapse into another Monday
like any other useless creature. Tiny teeth
of words, how will we ever know?

Mosaic Observations

Streetlights drone loud enough to reactivate
childhood's foothold again. Refrigerator
motor half a prayer, paint chips shatter
like cockroach shells, like wishes fluttering.
How calendars can entangle us so gradually.

Perpetual Suburbia

They teach you to iron linen napkins.
Seat male next to female to male
like that's all there is. Cocktail
voices reverberate past midnights.
Try to remember your thirsty heart.

Invisible Cobwebs

Earthmites teethe sharklike through
particles of sand, the bitter taste of day-
break. This nervous scratching in the night.
I bargain with quill-shaped mist, trying
to spin apart the twisted trembling.

Thursday's Child

Questions suspended from limbs dangling,
hushed phantoms circle attic roosts. Solutions
weave their dilemmas, upsetting this week's
schedule. We jealously follow wildflowers across
endless fields, seeking out our relentless dead.

Quicksilver Lilies

Baby squirrel curled broken, arms clawed
out against earth rocking. Eyes open
I brace myself in sleep. Rosehip brambles
shred raw an opaque glimmer of summer-
time. Shattering gossamer, silencing mist.

Sassafras Meadows

Sycamore's unearthly branches penetrate
haze, peeling back nerves of velvet mountains,
anything you couldn't leave behind.
Whatever you gave away to be loved,
you cannot tell where the sky begins.

Speculation Pavilion

Swollen pop of hollow reed, blushing
bones brake naked through bedrock crust,
rebalancing April somewhere between
anticipation and regret. Their emerald skins,
do they wonder what they came here for?

Asperity Dispensary

Jittery gusts reverberate spiraling waves.
Residues. Potash, hoof & horn meal,
the sky always falling a little. Soil-borne,
whole orbits circle this kaleidoscopic
afternoon. What will you take with you?

Harlequin Taproot

Marbled iridescent like pastel layers inside
shells, the confusing truth of skeletons
unravels me. Yesterday's sonnets, tomorrow's
rain, translucent stories shimmering,
is this all I will ever know of you?

Revelation Commission

Eyes of specter, alabaster gulls. Invisible
illness' eccentric orbits buried inside marrow
of the unborn. Visualize networks, summer hands,
how even flowers' fragmented imaginations
and tumultuous alphabets can unhinge belief.

Necessary Calendula

Ignore secret arrangements, what everyone
agrees this month. Carnelian pyramids
of bone, beach towels folded in twilight,
even unloved toddlers hum lullabies. Don't
wait until your body's compass has crumbled.

Honeysuckle Jasmine

Purple dirt drunk with August, planetary
revolutions etch glistening ribbons around
Jupiter, tearing apart some ancient weathered
chart. A cardinal plummets to the ground
like fallen fire, reinventing the darkness.

Innumerable Halos

After the full moon, corals unleash spores
into underwater snowstorms. Cheetahs and
wild dogs stalk their prey. Nocturnal migrants,
singing warblers streak past lunar splendor
while scientists count vanishing silhouettes.

Captive Harvest

No longer anybody's daughter, I drift
weightless over bedrock. Fragile labyrinths,
hindsight radiates next to my trembling
core. Clutching bundled words, I stumble
forward, neck frozen between beak & wing.

Bittersweet Discernment

In the hot glow of arc-shaped shine from
runaway stars, I dream-fly downstairs
toward the perfume of his cherry
tobacco. This drunken memory seducing
me into believing he'd returned again.

Shimmering Crossbow

Following seasons, I wander bedrooms,
recite the weekdays, monitor consonants
to tame undulating doubts. Rituals of
weather, I scavenge seashells & marrow,
salt for fires to divert every hostile mirror.

Latticed Partitions

Sirens pulse to a fury, then pale.
Ripped crimson silk of danger
tunnels into stillness. Half daughter
half swallow – if only I could
tie down the corners of the air.

Between Stepping Stones

Crickets tremble close to the earth,
hunger that brings me home,
a yearning no one can release.
Wash me in this. If you give
me the words, I will listen.

Ethereal Refractions

Gather honey roots and starfish, forbidden
deviations, the infinity between atoms,
circumference of each moment. Hungry
beaks crave rain. Eagles grasp claws, swirling
endlessly downward. Can you hear the waltz?

A Contagion of Miracles

Bring birds. Search out every microscopic
particle. Blossom-shaped, sunlight spirals
in through louvered glass ceilings. Persuade
the vertebrae to grow gradually back, past
all the boundaries we'd ever believed in.

Divisions of Solitude

Shallow sheets creased white, we dream
apart the length of days. Trace remote
outlines of plants through a thousand
gardens until the road becomes clear.
Nothing could be more now.

Fireworks of the Field

Whirl in embroidered linens by river's edge
as if it were yours. Butterflies glitter among
corn, bottlebush, soy, tonguing opalescent
wings. Weaving filaments, unexpected
colors everywhere into a flickering chorus.

Seagrass Airship

Scatter regrets into the rushing waters. Falcons
soar midair, interlacing transparencies to mate.
Locking talons, they gyrate free-fall toward
the blissful intersection of heaven/ river/
morning. Unspooling the untamed heart.

Space Capsule Chronicles

Silver halo of skin, humans silhouette ebony
against solar eclipse. Pilot past yellow umbrellas,
cantilevered constellations, blossoming
glass-cloud spread & elliptical galaxies –
until you can unlock forgotten secrets of breath.

Civil Twilight

Saturday sundown, headlights glimmer
into parkway's still blue mirror. Incremental
shadows of the dead, Father's hand gently
caresses my forehead. *You do me wonders*,
he whispers, before he disappears again.

Continuing Thanks Always To:

My mentors at Drew University, Master of Fine Arts in Poetry: Judith Vollmer, Mihaela Moscaliuc (for her above&beyond-the-call support), Aracelis Girmay, Joan Larkin. Thanks to Michael Waters, Alicia Ostriker, Sean Nevin for their special help. To Directors of the Drew University MFA in Poetry, Anne Marie Macari, Mihaela Moscaliuc and Sean Nevin. These and the residency poet-teachers, all who helped to bring me to the place I'd always wished for and could never find.

Thanks to those who continue to create communities for support, growth, connection, enchantment. With love and thanks to the literary communities that have sustained me:

The beloved fellow student-poets of the Drew MFA in Poetry program, who continue to create magic in the world. With appreciation for special help from Jane Seitel.

The St. Mark's Poetry Project, a glorious incubator. My teachers Bernadette Mayer and Alice Notley. For the thriving, spinning neighborhood poet-friends that created a special world to live in, at a special time.

The Poetry Center at Passaic County Community College, Distinguished Poets Reading Series and their workshops with luminous visiting poet-mentors.

To Writers in the Mountains' exciting, ever changing and growing literary community. To Simona David for sustaining it. To Leslie T. Sharpe. With grateful love and ongoing thanks to my students whose brilliant devotion and learning continues to inspire and teach me. To Sharon Israel for her ongoing help and support.

The Poetry Barn and its wonderful gathering of writers. To Lissa Kiernan, visionary founder. To Lissa Kiernan and Tina Barry for their insightful feedback.

To Geoffrey Nutter for teaching numerous ways to break apart thought-language to discover something more true. To the glowing international community of poets and their thrilling words.

To Angela Kelly who encouraged my jagged-raging sparks when the rest of the world required lady-like essays. To Ralph Pettie who unblinkingly taught college-level poetry and Shakespeare to eleven-year-olds.

To Ruth Wilson, who started us out with loving fairness. Now at 104 years old, she posts articles on Facebook on Brain Health and the Beauty of the World. Still a beacon to us.

Thanks to:
An embracing town with a Post Office that gives "good luck rubs" to outgoing poetry manuscripts. Thank you Sharon.

The gracious Phoenicia and Pine Hill Libraries for their beautiful spaces that understand us and house friendship and learning. The ongoing support of dear friends and the Morrison family. To Michael. To Fannie Petrovsky Taylor. For Laurie's generous help. To Nesha, Judith Singer and Penny for always believing in me.

To Melanie Gendron for her devoted work on the book design.

To my Publisher, Diane Frank, for her inspiring support and encouragement. In the past. And now.

About the Author

Anique Sara Taylor's chapbook *Civil Twilight* is Winner of the 2022 Blue Light Poetry Prize. Her full-length poetry book *Where Space Bends* was published May 2020. A Pushcart Prize nominee, her work's appeared in *Rattle, Common Ground Review, Adanna, Stillwater Review, St. Mark's Poetry Project's: The World, Earth's Daughters, Cover Magazine, The National Poetry Magazine of the Lower East Side* among others and widely anthologized. Her first chapbook *Poems,* is published by Unimproved Editions Press.

Taylor has co-authored works for HBO, Scholastic, Simon & Schuster and a three-act play performed by Playwrights Horizons and Williamstown Playhouse. Her Holocaust poem "The Train" was 2019 finalist in Charter Oak's Award for Best Historical Poem. *Where Space Bends* in earlier chapbook form was chosen Finalist by both Minerva Rising and Blue Light Press in 2014 Chapbook Competitions. In 2015 *Under the Ice Moon* was chosen Finalist by Blue Light Press.

Taylor teaches/taught Creative Writing for Benedictine Hospital's Oncology Support Program, Bard LLI, Writers in the Mountains. She holds a Poetry MFA (Drew University), Diplôme (The Sorbonne, Paris), Painting BFA (Highest Honors/Pratt), Drawing MFA (Pratt Institute) and a Master of Divinity Degree. She studied Literature at Antioch College and Poetry at St. Mark's Poetry Project with Alice Notley, then Bernadette Mayer. She's been a regular at Wallson Glass Poem-making Sessions with Geoffrey Nutter.

www.ingramcontent.com/pod-product-compliance
Lightning Source LLC
Chambersburg PA
CBHW031219090426
42736CB00009B/982